Mannequin Rising

Mannequin Rising

ROY MIKI

VANCOUVER | NEW STAR BOOKS | 2011

NEW STAR BOOKS LTD.
107 — 3477 Commercial Street
Vancouver, BC V5N 4E8   CANADA

1517 — 1574 Gulf Road
Point Roberts, WA 98281   USA

www.NewStarBooks.com
info@NewStarBooks.com

Copyright Roy Miki 2011. All rights reserved. No part of this work may be reproduced, stored in a retrieval system or transmitted, in any form or by any means, without the prior written consent of the publisher or a licence from the Canadian Copyright Licensing Agency (Access Copyright).

Publication of this work is made possible by grants from the Canada Council, the Department of Canadian Heritage, the Province of British Columbia, and the British Columbia Arts Council.

Cover design by Mutasis.com
Using an image by Roy Miki
Printed on 100% post-consumer recyled paper
Printed and bound in Canada by Gauvin Press
First printing, April 2011

LIBRARY AND ARCHIVES CANADA CATALOGUING IN PUBLICATION

Miki, Roy, 1942–
    Mannequin rising / Roy Miki.

ISBN 978-1-55420-056-6

    I. Title.

PS8576.I32M28 2011   C811'.54   C2011-901122-0

Contents

Tokyo Evening	3
Three Takes on Culture	5
Vestigial	7
Scoping (also pronounced 'Shopping') in Kits	9
A Walk on Granville Island	51
Viral Travels to Tokyo	73
Half Dozen Haiku Like	101
That Tree	103
Today	104
Willing to Change	106
Identity	107
Prosthetic Politics	108
AM Berlin	109
A Nagasaki Day	110
Tempus in Siegen	113
Early Morning in Taipei	115
Raw Data / Kyoto	117
Flight to Kamloops 9 / 9	119
Acknowledgements	120

In memory
Glen Gore-Smith

Tokyo Evening

for Grace T

Long ago he arrived from a distant land
with nothing but cultural baggage

Everything wore the sheen of overwritten
landscapes wrong from the outset

By slipping in and out of coffee houses
he soon began to re-orient himself

To the vibrant maples set alongside the
towering bluer than blue yuletide tree

Which frame set off no reminiscences
no calendric retrievals whatsoever

(Yet who is that white haired old guy
scribbling away in his little notebook?

In the motley line of passersby in the
window the cell phones blink in tune

They do not note his wobbling hand
shaking leaf-like in a soft evening breeze

The young radiate evanescence in attire
with a rainbow hue bursting through

You had to pay close up attention or
the slip cover would be blown away

Sure i fought against the slippage
when the anchors gave way to

Swallow this and swallow that but
don't forget where you came from

All the truths compiled in a list do
not add up to a usable commodity

Estrangement always has its loyalty
and turnkey days when we start over

As aging kindles kindlier abstractions
that sprout in grey matter once again

Three Takes on Culture

for Michael B

1

We came out the other end
strangely refreshed like browsers

Check out the linkages if you
want a slide down nascent codes

But hey rapids ripple down spine
in a tolerance to dine on my lungs

These wagers foretell the methods
of monitors with their chips down

2

The driver in the truck alongside
the bus doesn't look at the road
as wheels turn of their own accord

Some days it all works that way and
even students who don't ask questions
sit on their hands and wear the ink well

Larissa said in Taipei four channels in a
row broadcast buddhist priests chanting
right next to the all night porn channel

That's culture for you the body and spirit
after all these years still trying to contact
each other across the ornery digital divide

3

I think i know nothing then someone
shouts look here your feet are on fire

It's that nomadic verb found only in
dispatches lodged in palpable tines

Striking postures that fuse in fiery
dichotomies with the flush of roses

These days the pledge subscribes to
clashes with local fashion standards

Rumours in the gait of knee bending
when the second hand on its circuit

Confirms the health of the local in
the spectrum of its splintered ends

Vestigial

for Fred W

The notebook lost or left in the seat fold
took on the flue of history. All the drafts
that spoke of disappearing acts. All the
runaway words never to be retrieved.

The highway at least remains in forward
mode. Cruising on local bravura the
driver set his sights on the road while
the captive scooters on the passing semi
were uncaught in the lens. With the sweep
of his hands the scattered fields turned
into the dream of other landscapes.

> For instance the prairie road
> of his childhood as a wager
>
> against the vacant air of the
> side vents. The hot air and
>
> the cruel thirst on the bicycle
> still only halfway to Selkirk.
>
> To stand later where hands
> in the asylum window wept
>
> to see the tumbling outside.
> What he wagers as the land
>
> escaped again.

Remember the guide in the 228 museum breaking her
spiel when she got to 1895? This island seen as
so valueless it was ceded forever. All that matter

compressed in the palm of her hand. What does
it mean to move beyond it? What could it mean?

The strands of the electrical networks quiver
in an artificial breeze. It was all manufactured
for the benefit of posterity. Do we get it?

All hell bent loose on narrative devices. He
was raddled by what was lost in an instant.
Memory buckled in the faint hope of retention.

Surely the betelnut beauty on the roadside
in her glass enclosure spells the middle way.

Her reflection in the light of the bus window
transports him by ripple effect. The compacted
dream of locomotion the song without the singer.

Could it happen to me? Am I a social machine?
Do the buttons pushed on my retina trigger
insular buffer zones on the run? Should I ask
why the green hedges around the tables in the
mall are fake?
              Personally he was not averse
to a comely capitalist touch of faith but please
don't touch the back of this memory at least
not now on this road from Puri to Taipei

Scoping (also pronounced 'Shopping') in Kits

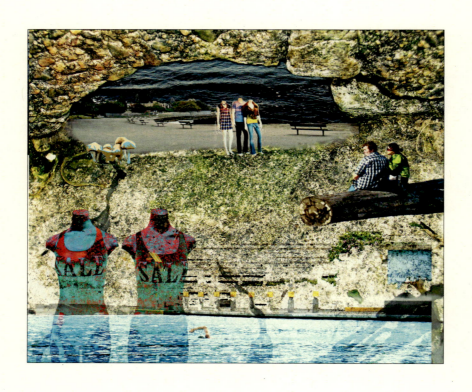

❦ There are more fealties than
one can safely stock in the store

Pedestrians ingest waves that one
receives as wet wheels leave the curb

Allowances on balance percolate
the membrane and tweak the otherwise

soft core of the lovers whose dials
turn towards the curvature of the

spinal nexus where the conflagration
of ruses blend into the ruffled hedges

whose resistances can ameliorate bevies
of stories left untold in the weathervane

The inverse ratio of production costs left
the mannequin speechless for the first time

The communication channels in the nest
of cavities make truce with a network

of pinhole cameras that admit the light
into recesses of double or nothing respite

∴

❦ The mannekins must share
foreknowledge of the rise
and fall of human desires

Their glances flit and sway
as each word in lip synch
nudges up against another

We think we are sentenced
in heated exchanges that
make creases in their postures

But that only supposes that
each nod has found its place
in a balanced basket of goods

The ripe fruit vegetables and
vintage wines in their adept
hands take place in the move

The dream in their presence
makes as it filters unsaturated
along spiraling back waters

What did the groove then
signify for you? What in the
spectrum of still shots came

Off as fake and artificial as a
wily summer breeze wafting
through the montage of frames?

We are consumers get used to
it we are here because you were
there and there is always a here

That brings fear of trembling to
the daily born exits that oft call
to the pause in the amber light

🜂 The scop in shopping
tumbles off the tongue

The inveterate creases
complete the off rhyme

How the poet survives
across zones in market

conditions such as this
depends on the allergic

reaction to the diction
that nary a breeze blows

A forest of sighs awaits
the feigned underclass

of commercial linkages
or transmissions in a lay

lingual operative on hold
such shadow boxing binds

the hop in hoping that
comes down to the wire

• •

❧ Must have been the kit
with spare parts of speech
that scraped the basin

Amicable as proverbial
winds that rattle cages
and smoke out each

Casual spell tossed in
a grammar as mellow as
melons boxed for a ride

Hide and go seek the sack
of flighty winds that trail
those spectacles of consent

Those in the parade so long
their leggings tie the media
fanfare in knots of nodding

When even the manikins on
duty know the conjunctions
do not placate the bellyache

Witness the rank file of those
disaffected in the enchanted
forest with rattling sabres

Show them the unmanicured
nails the implants that hail us
from beyond the artless dunes

Show them the fossil in the lye
or the eye burn that blanches
the domestic solace of news

∴

for Ashok M

🌿 The rising action of shrugged shoulders
The confluence of matched footsteps
The route of the induced visitations

In these instances the call of the social
fails to meet the watchful standards
of the fashion police on patrol

The workmen gloves fell in a fitful mirage

The passersby glowed in uneven tints

The media attributed these effects to the
downturn in the consumptive habits
of the neighbourhood rodents

Affixing blame on the fence rot
necessitated the move of an identified
family of squirrels to more restricted
quarters at a two block remove from
their sheltered ancestral traceries

'These are wondrous times,' one witness
was heard saying, 'no words adequately
inscribe the engineering of bodies modeled
on such a destitute superstructure of beliefs.'

This vial is only full of a patented truth serum

This idea fought its way in the rush hour
only to be sabotaged by a dull market day

This mollifier worked overtime all month
only to be replaced by the offshore version

∴

🍂 We are always at a loss when it comes
to the question of vision whether it is
better to fasten on a figure that passes
for optimal apprehension or to flatter
the turnabout in the inclination by dint
of resistances that make for patience

The patient is one who awaits the
ministration of a healing touch who
absorbs the turbulence of cells (phones
too) between the crustacean ensemble
on the rocks and the walks along the shore
as the body of water poses for the snapshot

I slid down the face of the intersection with
no regard for warning posters except for
the otiose sounds carrying the refrain
of the rumour mills with all their tell-
tale operations led by the fierce tenacity
of a nose ever close to the window dressing

Balk if you will or if you don't show me a way
to chalk up the losses to the prescience of
the mannikin who leaps out of the frame
breaking the mould for the typecast role
as a hanger on or even a model minority
breaking the synergetic bonds wide open

• •

for Louis C

❧ 'Could commodities speak we would say:
our use value may be a thing that interests
men. It is no part of us as objects. What belongs
to us is our value. Our natural intercourse as
commodities proves it. Now listen how we
speak through the mouth of the economist.'
Do you not detect in the slow motion of his
lips the slippage from the warm body to the
past tension of never being recalled for duty?

It is only a human thing you say but note the
recourse in our speech to the natural intercourse
of value for burgeoning exchanges that upset
the apple art as you say with no pun intended
the pun being reserved for superfluous occasions
that spell the gloom of market indices in the rush
to embrace the dizzy passages on billboard screens

'Could commodities speak we would say:
our ruse value may be our interest producing men.
It knows particles as objectives. Your nationalized
discourse of commodification rues it.' Now speak
how we listen through the dearth of domestic value.
In the turn of a phrase, 'must for reclining mountain,'
the land (i should have said hand) has been known
to yield graftings for fool's gold the yellow pearl that
once haunted the economic dreams of thing makers

It is useless to frown on the upstart conniving of
things that pay no heed to human truisms and tamper
with the ciphers binding performance to productivity
graphs and other domains in the kingdom of statistical
averages that cut our air tubes for discretionary ends
when we breathe value on the tips of branches

Should commodities speak we could say:
hey loosen up on the valet who imitates manly
interests alone. It is as partial as others. What longs
to be free of ruse value. Our nature as commodities
precedes us. Now fess up to the tricks of the trade
as the poet says 'the wet playing field is a testy mountain
that sinks back into the sea' or consider the circular
routes that turn on a dime and add up to the branch plants
that shed their leaves as signs of altruism for the mute earth

. .

❦ Such chemical agitators that forecast
the vacillation of nerve fallouts

Such warnings that stockpile
fuel for the rise in global pullouts

Such bends in the bottom line emit
symptoms of fondled merchandise

There in the embedded baits
prolong the rinsing of borders

The coursing of staged crafts
proclaim a mannequin inhabitation

Do we then mourn the dead or do
the dead scorn the memory of passing?

If the body all decked out in its strut
succumbs to the caress of the enemy

Who then hails the prancing pinball
striking the chord setting off the rush?

When the politicos banter about loyalty
border honour border courage border

The market for ipods skyrockets in
the lush muffle of currents on the fly

Find yourself before this glassine finish
when the reflectors on duty work overtime

• •

for Glen L

🌿 I was brought up on
streets where tongues
were forever wagging

The strain on the solar
plexis wore manifests
in the latest trends

Though washed jeans
on display spoke out
of lavender days

Under the eavesdrop
what got summoned
were forgotten strains

Like worn out pics
slipping on new duds
in the model race

I forever got brain
storms of insolvent
pardons on standby

As the unwashed soles
of trampling indices
muttered in unison

∙ ∙

❦ Drawn as they were to a flagrant
disregard for protocol and decorum

Alert to the dancer whose buoyant
tensility crouched in the outer ear

All the freed messenger pigeons lined
the store window as vested lookouts

'We hear you' sounded an exchange
of root pointers on the old pathways

They swayed on command and cooed
against the thought of new fashions

So that flutter found roots to citizens
in the late afternoon urban slumber

At the edge of the timer the dancer
took refuge in the gauze of eyelids

Like secular waves the windowsill
of receptors called to the strollers

In such synch the seismic portals
absolved the mirror of its resolve

• •

🍂 Did you notice it was impossible to distinguish between glass and mirror, or was it the mirror defect that the experts talked about?

The determination, in that instance, coincided with glances deflected on the concave surface of a voice box but one that had no speaker or at least a throat according to biological usage.

The thermometer registered a voice print with numerical values only known to forensics as they are wont to say in the media.

   • •

🌿 This one would not always
tell which layer precedes
and which one turns the key

How we buzz one another as
interlocutors who don't have
a way home except by way
of intercoms that are set to
distribute values across the
template of aboriginal change

Shifting range as the weather
balances social goods against
the pull of tidal encumbrances

Call them the ornery doubts of
makers lamenting the slowdown
call them the surplus of cells in a sea
of forgetting call them the market
miscues that are remembered as
local conflations of the good news

..

❦ *"Researchers find no seaweed and therefore no health benefits in Lululemon's Vitasea line of clothes. The Kitsilano-based Vancouver company has claimed that Vitasea contains 23% SeaCell, a fibre made from seaweed, which makes its material 'antibacterial, moisturizing and de-stressing for the skin.' Despite this breaking news, Lululemon customers are unfazed. 'I don't care if there's seaweed in my clothes, as long as they fit me right,' said one satisfied customer. The dip on the company's share value soon disappeared, and reports say it might even climb on the heels of the controversy."*

Is a lulu
a lemon

Is a sea
a skirt

Is a weed
a skin

Is a commodity
a companion

Is a patent
a belonger

Is a brand
a friend

Is a lemon
a lulu

Is a stock
a lotto

Is a lulu
a being

Is a store
a commune

Is a window
a scribe

Is a frame
a blame

Is a choice
a ruse

Is a person
a mobile

Is a rift
a gain

Is a meaning
a verb

Is a fund
a mental

..

for Hiromi G

🍃 If the manakins
could read lips
they would keep
their thought
probes a secret

No telling what
would become
of their lore
in the hands
of their makers

No telling what
logs would make
when the defence
has been such
stellar quietude

No telling what
winds stir what
quantum motes
register what fore
sight gives warning

See the audacity of
appropriation has
a history of pock
marked insignias
with sorry origins

See we ride only those
waves that breach the
shore line / tell us who
we become in the bubble
wrap of our beholders

• •

❦ Blending in eases the burden
of having that digital moment
when the screen of resistance
gives way to the particulates

The decibels unhinged from
reference in a hay day of lying
in the tall grasses by the drying
river bank all hallowed by the

Energy that emits the close by
entropic harmonies stirred in
the adept stairwell of saunters

I can breathe easier when the
undertow finds its airstream
and all the fluids in storage
awake to sibilant promptings

For once forget the injunction
to forget where the word rises
in the expectant dawn as the
yearning shells speak of altered

Courses of bondages undone
of strident voices put to bed
of billowing sails that confront
the rule of thumb and benumb

Those top down targeted digits
the trigger happy among them
whose stiletto heels turn sod

⁂

🌿 When the divisionary things break down
the only way down the rabbit hole is tinged
with goods. Some people get all the breaks.
Others have to wait until the crack of dawn.
We simmer in a catch basin of catch phrases.
The sliver of light is all we can go on. All
exhilarating dominance works the tempers
when turned to the perennial west winds.
The poet's escape route you say without
intending to harm the hard boiled (common)
core tricks of the trade. These days the skin
emits more 'out there' fears of redundant
resources to camouflage the unprecedented
raid on the naked and ravaged image. Records
of anonymous seizures shredded the falling
rhythms crying foul ball. Do you think all goods
are for you? All for you that the pulse pulsates?
That the hollow in the plexis is unforgiving?
That the homilies pile up like stranded truisms?
Signs of foreclosure in the subprime capital are
as menacing as the iron knee of greed feeding
on its own entrails. 'Happy trails to you' the
headline making composure of investor backlash.
'No pain no gain.' 'No sin no grin.' 'No blame
no fame.' The social goods are stacked. All bets
are off. No willows too much to manhandle. We
were off track as the announcer waived his voice
fee to expose his goods. You or i only wish the
rantings that blanket the public airwaves of
displeasure would yield the emergency of breath.

..

🌿 Are you suffering from compassion fatigue?
Does it bother you that you think you're
the only one who is not a victim? Do you
wake in the middle of the night and ask
why me? Then bingo hold on to your stirrups.
You've won an all expense paid cruise
through the discourse of your choice
with vocabulary tailored to your needs
and all perceptual states a projection of your
desires and your desires alone. A full message
massage is yours too if you please.

• •

❦ In one of those opportune seances
made memorable in commercials
we noticed the spike
in the demand ratio of mannikins
as if the sudden rise in the currency
were the equivalent of spiked water
that spurred their necessary
out of body consumer moment

The odometer set on the bank counter
next to their usual haunt
began to shimmy
when the crowd formed
more out of its curiosity
than old fashioned compassion

The speed of their liberation
infuriated the managers
even though nothing was audible
or visible or even recognizable
according to standard modes of measuring
dermal disturbances of similar types

In any case we were aroused
by their gazes that monitored
the micro-shifts in attention
releasing damp questions in
things no longer encased
in the packaging of human comforts

But tumbling out of flavour
the lateral mumblings of likeness
went awry in a bundle of reckless
indiscretions that willed our foot
steps out of their loose garments

∴

❦ All those clichés
like comings and goings
like the passing show
like the quick and the
lead foot the surfeit
not mine not amid
mind in the thickets
of its own making

Its sobriquet domain
some solace this
rain swept night

The leaves give up
their riotous flutter
and follow the lead
of the pedestrians
on the sidling parapets
wishing for the light
of the poet to make
do with the materials
at hand he was going
to say when the changling
patterns of the middling
ironies fell into the deep
sleep of consumption

They let it come to pass
let it follow the tract
the attractor factor
buzzed the interior
lobes of the truculence

At the viewing station
where the light dons

∙ ∙

❦ The synergies that make
the agora dense with fever
are not on tape but on tap
in the latest rendition
of our freewheeling
mediation called viral
in the tour guide's smoothie
lingo from the back of the bus

Whoever lingers in the passage
is bitten in the butt out campaign
aimed at the social informants
whose cell phone circumlocutions
were intercepted and translated
into policies that the man amongst
them ruled out of order out of
dispensation out of the pleasure
of the crown out of the envy of
humanoids out of the silence
of the hams out of the flora
flying in your face out of
the arms of membrane rip tides

∙ ∙

❦ Miniscule specks turned up beneath
the surface of common things setting
off forensic speculations that reached
into the folds of systems heretofore
unnamed in the routine procedures
that had come to enhance the daily

'If you follow the line of forethought
you get entangled in the nests of being'
was the slogan devised to foresee
the leakage between things as if
the things themselves were in
cahoots with the fine line threads

Elsewhere the footsteps were softer
as the cushions of the soles treading
so lightly on the cobblestones were
heard to mutter sweet jargon to one
another in defiance of the injunction
not to expose the frailty of the codes

The anxious as a measured conduit
of the common properties visible in
the haltometers erected in select sites
were known to resonate with bauds of
sound bites as the enflamed frame to
the garments of their distress signals

The affront has to do with copyrights
patents branding all the paraphernalia
that strip the doormat of its right not
to be trampled that chant 'mine mine
mine mine' in a post-historical rampage
that guns down the freeway all the rage

The feline qualities of this confined intensity
bear witness to a time and place that
dissolves even as it rasterizes the evening

stroll down the busy thoroughfares while
the buses come and go and the green grocer
quietly takes in the produce on the sidewalks

Such astonishment you say as you too get
absorbed in the digital non sequiturs that
enter the dream of the already blanketed sea

   • •

🌿 What expectation
standing there at
attention all day

What scream is
recognized as

a sign of the living

Go ahead let loose
a hurricance of vocables

• •

for George B

🍃 We often queried the early evening light
when the scents of another era courted
the maple branches canopying the street

A quiet snail about to cross the sidewalk
made for a parable in an otherwise loose
attempt to conjure the comfort of rhyme

The shoe store had all versions of designer
runners that the market could bear as I
looked down at the bathos of my own

There must be a designer body awaiting
on the other side of the makeshift percept
that came to mind and then exited stage left

The perspective of the sea in the distance
with the sky designed by power lines (don't
photoshop them out please, not until later)

The dissolve deludes us into thinking the
street is a coach that pulls into town at noon
bringing news of the war on other shores

The terror that contains error comes out of
the blue corridors where horsemen trample
the disappearing bodies on the other side

In the silence of the mannequin is the location
that reaches towards the latest buzzwords that
fork out more than monetary conflagrations

The tyranny of the commodity prods its arms
and torso to hang loose while the garments
hang tight on headlines unfurled in the doorway

The ink had already dried when the internal
combustion engines disseminated their gaseous
opulence as if the reeds could be so modified

Beads of a rampant hoardiness marked
the boundaries of designer ramparts that
allocated symptoms to rueful dispatches

The restive figures rustled the leaves that
forgot to cling to branches in the time taken
for the snail to make it to the other side

• •

A Walk on Granville Island

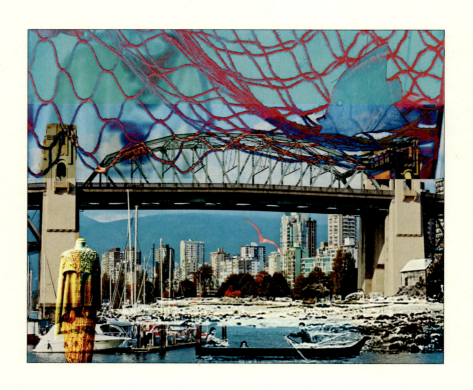

🕯 Today the rambunctious gulls (above)
squawk about the resurrection of sky
lines / the hallowed out angles that
festoon our gregarious sentiments

The social but paranoid crows (below)
discourse on the lowly virtue of hand
picked local produce / feigning the
trendy bundle of crossed purposes

Once the sprays of memory juices
breach the already docile insights
of the forlorn cultural critic eating
concepts on the planked boardwalk

We squeak an effervescent discontent
as throaty bellows from the pilings
pay no attention fees to ransack
the shafts of light for an audio feed

One day this land is yours to alienate
Son / lest you forget these planks kick
about the inflated stature of / well
statutes and their blandished comforts

Remember the price of submission
in the salted visage on the promenade
and its 'not for display' old footage

∴

🍂 These consumers in motion
have no name tags no ids
to drift off to dreamland
in a carnivalesque pitch
that cannot be notated

It could be that a walk
along the seawall arrests
the detached thought
keeps at bay the resilience
of thighs and the canvas

Let the rain mosey down
the waterproof garments
in a canopy of charms

It's not so foolish to stoop
over the edge of the pier

Not so foolish to brain
storm the refracted light

• •

❦ Whereas this cluster of shoppers with
draw hope from dangling pronouns

And whereas this bridge that con
joins resists the run on the sentence

And whereas this designated place
mat is tight lipped on migratory commas

And whereas this market erected in mid
stream feeds on the veins of creeks

And whereas this not for sale make
shift canoe replicates the idea of passage

And whereas this reverse of water con
flates the drainage of seductive fillings

And whereas this island stands as trade
mark to the buoyancy of socialite codes

Let the rhetoric flip its blissed nominals
on the farthest reaches of its distemper

Let chains of recurrence picket all
the wickets on the chagrined boardwalk

Let fruit (o raspberries) in basketry
collapse into circuits of belonging

Let no wreckage patent the pillage
or haunt the glowing in the village

••

❦ Only yesterday, yes only
yesterday the bottle necks
were safely maintained

Now someone called long
haul seeks to bottle entropy
as a brand to die for

You can never have enough
of odds (and evens) on the
shelf life of security tickets

The exchanges grow paths
integral to quantum aptitudes
wherein percepts intercept

Now those subcutaneous
neuronic nudges seasonal in
industry what's in or out

In the latest market crash
capital shot itself in the
foot registered as a hit

So pectoral outlet in a fit
accrued new butt lines to
reconnect the ancient dots

All claritas the prophecy
etched in the mouth
that feeds this island

∙∙

for Rita W

🍂 If you were to walk
off this landmark pier
and hold your pose
for a sidelong glance
what would it look
like on the descent?

Where are the trap
doors that snap
shots of the harbour
in its comely doldrum?

How to explain to the
kids feeding the pigeons
the etymological drift
of the Arterial Highway?

Look it up in the dream
almanac of memorabilia
in the lost causes that
bewitch the clichéd ambit

There's the still born fancy
of one Jack Price (yes Price was
his name) who campaigned
on the slogan that 'real progress'
would entail the removal of all
the waters under the bridges
and voila so much real estate
to boot for Jack Price 'False
Creek is nothing more than a filthy
ditch in the centre of the city'

We could all be skate
boarding on False Creek
and our civic parties
would be free of Dragon
Races and regattas of all
sorts wouldn't ruin our
slumbering condo moment

That viscous wind blown
video of pliant asphalt
might have been a
seawall of the rapt mind

In any case do you remember
the lovely Mrs Percy Nye?

She who in 1891 reported
'False Creek was so quiet
on a Sunday we could hear
the Indians singing at their
services on the reserve as far
as our place on English Bay'
from our place on English
Bay 'we used to sit on
the shore and listen'

So let's rendezvous the
appellation of muskrats
smelts salmon crabs clams
the glossary of eco-friendly in
the chemical bath of this inlet

Or would you rather wash
your hands of this stuff?

∙ ∙

🕯 Why not embouchure the fashionable
the ripe and ready the oh my god i must
have that armature as if it could abandon
us to the zero in their designs on you

It's a shame to go disheveled in our
street clothes without proper witnesses
for the youtube momentum of our
fleet transplants across global monitors

Come to think of it why not come to my
senses with legs outstretched for the island
of fair trade without those nasty flashpoints

But please note the improv clique of pigeons
of all ages bobbing biometric heads for seeds
displacing the frenzies inside the camera lens

Now of all times are the conduits that raise
eye-brows among the consumers without license

You got it when the opportunity strikes is
a fire drill but do not panic you don't want
to drive the whole market to rachet wait for
the season to discern what rot is all about us

We are left to ponder why those
tulips grow only on that side

Past the connaisance
Past even the watchful tides

..

🍂 Every time we break a resolution
when an impulse to utter flourishes
I urge without adequate compensation

The swell wave made by the oceanic
histrionics by the mannequins are sold
through the layaway on hold

It's a matter of belief in the panorama
around the mobile shoppers

You believe then or
when I informinate you

Let us go then you and you and you
before the market closes all we have
are the track suits on our backs each
gut wrenching outfit recorded for
posterity on our minds bent to wards

Organic silences weigh in at double
the rate of those inflected with pesticidal
harmonic brand through subtle alternatives

Mannequins need to consider the delicacy
in these fades of fission friendly (FFF)
when to hold shape is utterly composure

..

❧ When we tripped when the ocean
floor played tricks on our gait
when his gaze dissolved when
he fell into the s-shaped moment
when it was that time stood still

Why do clichés come to the rescue
why do we ask are you okay does
your watch need to be reset why
are we beset by these disarming
circumlocutions why does the
chain link fence signify time
ill spent when we thought well
spent in the rear view mirror

Small arterial rivulets service
nutrient creek excess seguys

His skin a resin akin to perforate
parcels of land reclaimed to feed
the maws of industrial seasoning

All the bargains of truce pastures
of slopes in staged decline in finagle
with bated breaths taken on the lamb

Cuticles abrasive corrosive solvent
salacious undertows beauty filial

An alloy in the market retention awash
in templates down the rain filled crevasse

Don't hallow me out say let the ravine
rave on say consign the completion to
the ulterior motive say even handed
rifts are best left stranded in sedges

Don't stockpile the washed out effect
and don't believe me when i say
sediment roams like no other

Have faith that shallow
has no low shell to squander

The rum in the stocking
packs a mean punch

Lines that say fallout are
beset by twangs of silt

..

❦ Do you believe that all these
waters have not been charted?

These instruments on the dock
are tracking devices

They barely hold together
under intense scrutiny

Once upon a time one could
say there was an all purpose
supermarket in this solidity
that could not have been

For instance here in the crook
of a water colour scenario
a dissolve of say brown and/
or blue with a smidgen of grey
in the hand me down clouds spoil
the mandarin oranges pyramidically
poised to capture our fancy this

i wonder about the starlings that
congregate around the passengers
who dole out food substances freely
with an elan usually associated with
those with gifted bodies and minds

..

for Ayumi K

🌿 *Where would we be
without the sea?*

*Likely, not here
Or like, not here*

*It was the sea carried
George Van Couver into
English Bay in June of 1792
exactly 300 years after
Columbus' historic voyage*

English Bay lay in waiting
for Couver and his sweet ship
June who was descended from a
set of numbers, likely the code
for a lucky charm bracelet

Did Couver and Columbus then
meet on the seas in a virtual
space of mutual refinement?
Exactly 300 years is a dead give
away for the tags voyage and historic

The question why Couver was born
and why in Vancouver of all places
is a lacunae in the fold up tale

But listen, *mariners charted
our globe for us*

(Much gratitude

*Remade our world
from flat to round*

(More gratitude

*Ushered in the centuries
that have given us today's
'global village.'*

Now we're getting fusion
with the centuries now we're
getting baseball teams bowling
leagues real estate companies
the whole shebang all at once

We mean the *sea trade has forged
the links that unite the earth's
nations in a single marketplace.*

Those mariners mapped
the seas that joined the nations
that sprouted from earth to market
to market to choose a transgenic pig

Sorry not today May of 2010
exactly 97 years after Snauq
villagers were uncharted
by Couverites on speed

Too much village is infectious
was the headline in the daily

••

🌿 What was later identified as toxic soup bore marked
resemblances to the expectations of the research plan
(see study commissioned by the city fathers circa 1916

Not only were the radial demarcations in contradiction
to ascribed emotive qualities of the imagined endgame
the sheets of slogans let loose a corpus of the margins

That era before the markets for water sumptiousness
were measured in the purer facets of a dialogue
that relied on strings of overworked adjectives

The island arose out of the mud of flats that had
weathered the doxa of fervent breaths for generations
before the arrival of telescopic plumes running on empty

When rumour oft told of breached fortresses / ramparts
and the logic of logs that lined the pockets of
diehard coalitions that sought the jewel of the inlet

Enter then the fillers those with ingenuity and where
with all to take chance on the limb to turn water
into territory into the modal call of the ages

(See the reference to historical markers such as
plaques benches inscriptions archives and the
word of the mouthful that speaks of enterprise

Once mellow times were all the rage except in instances
the degree of want looked westward in blood lines
governing a passable living before the final clinch of rest

Due diligence one said was the watchword little known
to work wonders on those who can taste the doable last
resort of the virtual lovers who cast their nets out dubiously

• •

Viral Travels to Tokyo
for Kirsten M, Cindy M, Scott M, and Monika G

🌿 Viral must be chuckling all the way to the supermarket. Yesterday at Narita when the AC 3 landed a cadre of masked officials in blue hospital garb as in monitoring a contamination site swept us with an instrument geared to measure temperature levels. One poor soul trapped in its body was circled with red stickers and became in that instant the hot zone. The rest of us were ushered off with hand signals stirring the suspect air.

We are the guinea pigs the lowly relatives of the swine targeted for the global ruckus disseminating we hate to say it just like a virus that seeks a host (an us) to reproduce its kind. Colonies of restless sojourners bent on global migration to forge mobile identities.

In this surge of hybrid coalescence our bodies are conducive to being human or not. Viral as infrastructure finds voice in molecular networks in forms of 'social distancing.' Instead of shaking hands let's bump elbows and forget hugs and kisses. That's so pre-H1N1. Physical contact of any kind is so socially passé.

A new clothing line Virality features sleeves with nestled gloves when the need arises and a collar that sprouts a mask for near contact scenes such as in elevators where instant gratification is delayed. The fashion industry has gone gaga with the ripe possibilities of unheralded profits from this latest evolutionary phase of what has been dubbed viral globalization. A globalization all but invisible and dependent on a host of monitoring devices gone post-visual post-traumatic and tellingly post-pig.

turbulence zones
in on Tokyo's light

winding down clock
time it's already tomorrow

before today is done
the recuperation queries

who is that masked gaijin?

it follows that nothing
is irretrievable in the descent

Where is the hot seat located? Where does the wand seek to land? What if the thermal vane spins out of whack? The clipboards hanging on the inspectors are blank and look more decorative than rowdy. One seat over, K sees they've been tied over their shoulders, as if improvised, with some plastic rope with frayed edges. Hedge against the tide, so we suppose. What's with the goggles in the fractured light? We wear our metabolic suits in neutral colours for the duration.

❧ The bantering streets of Tokyo and my favourite
shopping stop Shibuya wear the shimmer of
new operatives that show viral has dalliance
on its side. The masked pedestrians approach
each corner as a task to be accomplished what
ever other terms like mutate enter the equation.

Distance only figures a desire for more intimacy.
Cheek to cheek lip to lip the others find a way
to make hay out of the breakdown in protocol.

When I first laid eyes on the mask we thought
out loud that the disguise was an outlaw fugul
arrangement made to measure for the influx
of a stream of consciousness not the old
fashioned kind but purposefully made for
our global fidelities. In the end it's the
same old body that slips through the net and
finds its own watering hole beneath the radar
of oblivious gazes. Don't get me wrong. The trick
is in the way the hands caress the tree branches
in the new interspecies mode of daydreaming.

who can read the insignia
of its intelligentsia network?

the face masks are a dead
give away that the forks in
its nodes of telepathy
are fluid and capacious

can you not hear the
chuckling in its wings?

this viral dispersion disproves
the untimely death of history

it's a stroke of genius

Seventy-five years later and Hachiko still waits, his loyalty all but forgotten in the heat of consumer movement. The viral overtures of the mannequins do not rustle the feathers of the pigeons. The friendly hearts at Shibuya stare into a hundred million cell phones.

❧ Tissue paper thin
thinner tissue of

Inaudible strangers
amidst the spectrum

Of strummers enfolded
in the mock orange

Style of cell phone
'manner mode' that

Hue and cry i can
recall only figments

Of each decade in
the templates of the

Side show slides the
retinue cross the retinal

what was that noise?

the intake of breath

a donation of sorts?

out of sorts

assorted?

all speeched out

The keitai or cell phone is so ubiquitous that the 'manner mode' or silent mode is normative. Texting is all in the course of a day. Playful characters, a host of emoticons, spontaneous photos, animated figures all make for a sumptuous digital escapade for consumers of all ages and temperaments.

❦ So much is left out
of the account as if

All details skipped
ahead of the recall

Where in the rapid
fire frames the train

Window makes is
the shelf life of i?

If the i in site is
befriended by ste

How much sweeter
can bathwater be?

The present fallows
the memoire in its

Tensile grip and
grime and gripe

Swishing the name
plate in a flourish

in korea town
the little yellow
melons wrapped
in cellophane on
styrofoam plates
are served up
to the customers
in the spendour
of the evening
only here
only here
only here
she said

🌿 From the walls of the shrine museum
the faces of the dead forever young
bear witness to a trail of notebooks

Of the young whose post memories
bear witness to the trail of blossoms
falling in the mirror of their gaze

The sanctuary a meeting fomented
in the ashen fables of formidable
auguries gone the way of petals

Fallen arches and the relics under
glass cases the rusty water cans the
gas masks the fateful model plane

Bear witness to the underside of the
gleam world in the exterior memory
of techno sounds the echo of echoes

Mournful is hardly a modifier for
the entranced sutures hanging like
mementoes that divine the wind's ill

we need to place
our mind inside
our mind so that
the rhythm takes
our voice

talk to me take
what the lips
gather in meeting

host turns
to host turns

Everywhere there are warnings against taking photos in the Yasukuni Shrine museum. Artifacts of the Special Defence Forces or the kamikaze ('divine wind') are laid out side by side in display cases. In this buffered place the vanquished become heroes, or in the words of the poem on a tapestry hanging in the theatrical light to hail the Yamato spirit or 'soul of old Japan': 'it is like the cherry blossoms / that bloom in the morning sun.' Following the young school children taking notes for assignments, I too scribble down what cannot be documented on my Canon camera.

❧ Ebisu light headed i
saw your long hair
trail the soft gust
up the stairs

45 years is not so
long i not belong as
finger points to me

The one long frame i
can long do without

You turn back to i

when cumulous clouds
flaunt their forms

memory wrought
in the sidelong
glance on the
path the rain takes
to the pavement

those horizonal streaks
turn out to be laughter

after all

This once modest station with simple entrance and exit sites has become a hub of pedestrian mobility. Up and down, down and up, each segment of this station enacts a serial poem. No kidding. When my attention drifted for a second from the espresso coffee I was drinking, I swear the material conditions of my consciousness were subverted by this consolation from the past.

❧ What foresight garnered across
benchmarks cannot be slipped
into the hip pocket on the way
to the airport. The dream augurs
as much as its lapses glitter with
the pride of ownership. Modest
mannekins quietly conceal the
opulence of the food mart
their hand gestures placating
while they direct the traffic
of onlookers. The heat made
their souls ache as the probe
inserted in their ears upped
the ante as they say on the
social veracity of the self
generated heat rising out of the
dream machine that made the
square of the station and its
every watchful Hachiko the
object of his attention. After all
he too radiated the mobility of
the viral instigation that had made
so much delay on the Tokaido Way.

        even up
        the eyes

        seek
        arches

        pine needles
        in that forest

I just happened to be glancing out of the side window when the heel of a young woman walking briskly down the narrow (back?) street snapped off and drifted away from her left foot. She quickly retrieved the (now?) stray heel and attempted to force it back onto her shoe. It kept falling off. For one moment she turned back, perhaps thinking that she should go back home (where?). She changed her mind and slipping the stray heel in her purse she put her shoe back on and continued walking, her heel raised to the exact level of the (new) phantom heel. No one will notice the missing appendage at Meguro station, I'm sure of it.

🍃 In a bid to outweigh itself Viral jumped the rails. The feat went unnoticed in the scientific community. Barrels of overture were heard tumbling over the falls. Wily roots of the translocal made for a daydream of origins and ends. The karada laden moisture a balm in the mist of ancient trads. We heard the uguisu sing for its breakfast and then held our conference outside the bounds of touch. The watch word was consumer beware as it was on the nether side. Viral is as viral does. The act speaks volumes in the absence of local references. Only the sell out of masks and the empty shelves where they had been bore witness to its ingenuity in such dire circumstances. Salut dear reader do not make hay in the season of tsuyu.

me guro

eye black
die cast

a road way
a blind alley

fore cast
fore paw

follow me
grow me

me guro

❧ A throng of crowds along
transit mirrors awash in
the sea fool of forget

Beware Lethe of critical
mass in the overflow
phenomena when

Monkeys wash sweet
potatoes in the salt
waters in their toes

Much more than a deluge
of cellular flourishes
come to pass in this

Late afternoon soft light
at Shibuya station where
Hachiko still keeps watch

In the hubbub of migrant
souls whose voices exit
the sentinel manikins

The still points in the
wobbling pivot of the
armature of the depato

one slipped
out of grace

one note slipped
between the covers

a bank of slipped
opportunities

slipshod ware on
secure airwaves

notice one didn't
slip over the hedge

ringed round with
slip stream dreams

🌿 We doubt that
the wheel turns

just because the
axle is greased

Top down postures
are so out of fashion

One blend stage wets
(whets?) the appetite

making it well nigh
impossible to forget

Half Dozen Haiku Like

for Powell Street Festival

For S

Keep on sweep talking the ground
as green twirlies sweep down again
O zounds! they're calling my name

A Recent Trip

What happens when he
got the H out of Utah —

Uta! Uta! cries the ah so
spry spirit of Kiyooka-san

Reel One

Stray dirt piles on stones
beside the stoic pot : squirrel
talk to evacuate the mind's plot

Sojourner

The scooter just missed him
hugging the lane fence — almost
Japanese is never enough

Eh? Go!

At the Meiji Gakuin university
guest house off the beaten path
of Meguro-dori one unsuspecting
poet encounters his first asagohan
sentence of the day, 'Please ask
caretaker when you need more lines.'

Lazy Haiku

Rain
drops

Pitter
patter

Rogue
sounds

Bow
ow

That Tree

> *The tree which moves some to tears of joy is in the eyes*
> *of others only a green thing that stands in the way.*
>   — William Blake, 1799, THE LETTERS

I say what is that tree doing in my right of way?

I mean what is that tree doing obstructing my face?

I say what is that tree doing to my block of time?

I mean what is that tree doing with its branches askew?

I say what is that tree doing with its trunk?

I mean what is that tree doing with its designer pose?

I say what is that tree doing with my consumer insight?

I mean what is that tree doing with the object of my affection?

I say what is that tree doing with my insider trading?

I mean what is that tree doing with its proliferation of buds?

I say what is that tree doing in the alley beside the overflowing bins?

I mean what is that tree doing crossing the street?

I say what is that tree doing with its hands up?

I wander what is that tree doing to my hindsight?

I sought what is that tree doing to my forethought?

I sink what is that tree doing to my wireless lapdog?

I pine what is that tree doing to my indigestion?

I mean what is that tree doing in my hip pocket?

I say what is that tree doing inside my head?

Today

Pretensions aside
     war is the failure of the
imagination

The breakdown in tor-
     rents of communication
unexpected yields

Specular rufflings
     those that mosey on up to
flirtatious cell lines

And habitual
     circuitry sustained
in the ravished heart

Its solace the fabular
     domicile of the consum-
er class / A wonder

Promulgated by
     media in love with
circular fancy

Fill the crevasses
     of our creature comforts to
suitcase the results

What sallies forth as
     our eyes glaze over on cue
hums a sublunar

Tune the riant crowd
      under the bridge emits an
echo of echoes

So that the flange view
      from the promontory reeks
of class privilege

It's so refreshing
      to know where you're going to
where you thought you've been

I mean the devil
      in the details
its untold quagmires

It's not obvious
      as you might assume beneath
the paper thin skin

Time to quiet the
      ghosts / Did you actually
shrink wrap it all up?

Willing to Change

What is that wisp
of mallow coiled
up on the mat?

A feline form
in dorm?

This question rises
from an unpatented move
that desire makes

as if a chosen one
were to balance one
fingerprint and another

muzzling up docile
imprints of shoreline
as waves of discourse

But is it improper
to say discourse
in this instance?

Do we need to seek
permission for such
acts of filling the void?

Or do we avoid rueful
memories of incarnation
by other means?

Some days phrases leap
and make their appearances
in the very vocabulary
they should have doused

Identity

That static noun with
so much encrustation

Even jetsam in the holds
of sand trapped ocean liners

Their whistle blowers hang
the nostalgia on wreathes

Under the latent carapace
where chamber voices

Follow the timbre of self
made stamp collectors

Such management itches
in the temperate loams

While flags wave in unison
at the alert border guards

Prosthetic Politics

for Larissa L

The power of crutches is so deceptive
Out of sight they bleed into the margins
Out of hand they assemble the social scene

As in this instance on the sidewalk
note the pattern or the way the feet sashay
to avoid the peg's unceremonial crunch

The feet I mean know not what dispossesses
them in the missed beat. Beyond the protection
of skin's integrity lie the folds of slights

You can say light's disposition if you wish
It also brings a defiance of grids and the pallid
demeanours cordoned to aid in traffic regulation

I even noted a swaggering followed by deft
physical graces that countered the militant airs
as if nothing could matter much less then

But stairways invoke the differences where
the flat rather than curved surfaces require
a concentration that exceeds the descent

Each step echoes the cultural equivalent of
a booster shot that produces the clairvoyance
of hierarchic eye contacts the splices of which
make gaijin instability a wonder to behold

Going by the book leads to vocal strain
and the worst sort of back pain imaginable

Mind you the blind steps reveal far more
blemishes than the clasp of band-aids

AM Berlin

Does the morning light
conceal as much as
it seeks to consume?

This earnest wake
of winged fears

We've been down the
road before lit flames
of passing figures

They are strangers in
the open courtyard who
sip coffee and mediate
the anxious ravens
he pondered all day

•

At the intersection
the bus stop with
its air of inter alia

A shelter of crowds
A meandering amongst

Bent on turning those
syllables over again

A familiar touch
of the diaphram

A Nagasaki Day

for Baco O

1

Does it matter if we
can't hear the inaudible
see the invisible?

So go buy me a muffled
horizon / Dress it
in kiddy corner turns

It always hails the most
unexpected of downpours

2

Since the shelters
were installed
the city wears

the look
of pleasure

of leisure
that cloaks

3

They wouldn't have
it otherwise

I thought i caught
the transition

No wonder
the arrangement
broke down

Blindfolded it
shimmered when

it could have
stood still

Back then

    4
It was quite
an ordinary day

the horses in
Goto-machi
clopped along

the streetcar
stopped in
Hamano-machi

and families ate
quietly in Ohato

    5
In the harbour
the boats at bay

the window wickets
with their signs
of glorious sites
lose their elasticity

as the typhoon's language
awaits translation

   6

I am only a
transfer point

an unreliable
witness to fashion

in a network of
waning apostrophes

Tempus in Siegen

for Mita B and Katja S

For whose benefit do the omniscient
bells toll in the now clasp of Siegen?

The seismic count resounds in each
muscle in the sway of thighs that
cross the ever whispering intersection

Set your useless watch as each temple
registers the tempus tender strikes

Even the lungs breathe in all deepest
measures as echo chambers in the
nether region of windowless frames

Counting down or up each interval
anticipates its upbeat waves in the brain
drain drawing on empty nested receptors

The scripters knoll a pilgrim's progress
to digress on how many words have you
and your backpack alleviated this day?

I too hone my tempus in the Siegen mall
the reckoning wreaks havoc in a well cured
insularity too used to being on the defensive

All tropes are costly she said as i turned the
corner and the mall door behind me left a
whiff of succor like sublime at loose ends

All the deciduous templates muffled close
ties beyond the strain of those intemperate
climes that coast a close circuit teleprompter

These bells spin diagnoses on the celestial
exploits of scopic devices that cannot be
detected by biometric infidelities that bring
a host of fortuitous fingerprints into play

Early Morning in Taipei

All along he thought
he understood until he
stood under the canopy.

Non-synchronous lines
so moist the earth gave
up secrets. The rain-
drops gathered on cars
in the graying dawn.

History's hollow
tunnel again the
slow boat to China.

The shake up in blame
routes (no reason) haunt-
ed him to no end.

I saw the scooter in
the beamed up showroom.

Curvilinear
all so malleable
neural indices
one level of skin

Print bore the datum
of incendiary
tongues of flames casting
the on-lookers (un-
recorded) in shades.

For goodness sake give
the guy a break he
only gathers moss.

The evidence tastes
like ironing filings
or was it filling?

He overheard the
question while he stood
in the virtual
island in the mid-
dle of the causeway.

Raw Data / Kyoto

for Smaro K

The weight of the stroll
     of youth culture along the Kamo
on this sultry night

Feathers brush against stone
     not randomly placed / Invoke
repetitive paths towards

temporal markers
     bodies laden with / My own
sticky fingers pinch

A weight that bears the
     shoulders / As if the sounds
drifting across the bridge

were heard melodies —
     Drowsy from too much to bear
hardly audible

Against the curtain
     of unrecognizable
intonations as

the night sidles through
     back lanes of barking voices —
trails aloft in hawk

Do think the time has
     come to abandon all hope
of retrieving the

weighted stones strewn re-
        distributed according
to rank files / The river

glitters against the
        rowdy outpourings in each
syllabic raiment

The crows earlier
        dropped their guarded postures and
regrouped only after

the young black cat slipped
        under the pilings / Tell me
more hesitations

stand alone releases
        motion me to get on with
it / Palpitate as

Implantations of
        bios as far away place
that admits error

Flight to Kamloops 9/9

My mother said dash-it
whenever she got angry

Strange how such a courtly
word could carry such punch

So now i look out the window
of this dash-8 and down there

The browning hills of kamloops
look like mounds of —

Oh excuse me
'deep deep earth'

Acknowledgements

Some of these poems were previously published in *Lexicon Radio*, *Open Text*, *Rampike*, *pH6: a book of haiku moods*, *Rocksalt*, and *West Coast Line*.

Thanks to the BC Arts Council for a much appreciated writing grant.

Thanks to Michael Barnholden and Nicole Markotić for useful last minute feedback.

Thanks to Rolf Maurer for his generous support, friendship, and excellent editorial guidance.